So This is Love

Book III

Oliver Forward

So This is Love
Copyright © 2024 by Oliver Forward

ISBN: 979-8895310342 (hc)
ISBN: 979-8895310328 (sc)
ISBN: 979-8895310335 (e)

All rights reserved. No part of this publication may be reproduced, distributed, or transmitted in any form or by any means, including photocopying, recording, or other electronic or mechanical methods, without the prior written permission of the publisher and/or the author, except in the case of brief quotations embodied in critical reviews and other noncommercial uses permitted by copyright law.

The views expressed in this book are solely those of the author and do not necessarily reflect the views of the publisher, and the publisher hereby disclaims any responsibility for them.

Writers' Branding
(877) 608-6550
www.writersbranding.com
media@writersbranding.com

Contents

A Quiet Moment With You 1

Comfort Me 2

For Some Reason 3

Give Me More 4

Honestly 5

I Can't Stop Myself From Loving You 6

I Could Never 7

I Feel Your Love 8

I Keep Reminding Myself 9

I Never Met a Dream 10

I Want You 11

I Want You Here 12

I'm in Love With You 13

I'm Madly in Love With You 14

Just One More Time 15

Listen to My Voice 16

My Tears 17

Only 18

Only If I Had Wings 19

Please Forgive Me 20

Set Me Free 21

The Bars of Love 22

These Emotions I Just Love 23

The One You Love Hurts You Most 24

The Sweet Voice 25

The Times 26

We Belong Together 27

What Will Happen Tomorrow 28

Will You Love Me 29

You Are Extremely Special 30

You Are My Thoughts 31

Your Forgiveness 32

Your Love Gripped 33

Your Love Was Born 34

A Quiet Moment With You

Can I have a quiet moment with you?
To talk about my love for you
The dawn of the day has approached
The doorbell of my unrestful heart
I have endless thoughts of not seeing your lovely face
I see these circles going around and around inside my head
I'm feeling so confused,
From the idea of not having your warm body
Having its lying next to mine
This shock has given birth to fear
Just the idea of not hearing your beautiful voice or seeing that Mona Lisa smile
Leaves me bewildered
How can I live without you?
I'm experiencing something that has a hold on me
Like a comet tide dancing up and down across the crystal sea
I have become a prisoner of my mental reactions
It is very difficult for me to find satisfaction
This is disturbing
Knowing I'm living outside of my comfort zone
Leaving me breathless
I've lost control of the day
I glanced into your demanding eyes
I've not been the same
Tell me, can I have a quiet moment with you?

Comfort Me

Comfort me when my tears will not wash away my sadness

Comfort me when I need a friend

Comfort me when life seems heavy

Comfort me when my finances do not match my bills

Comfort me when I'm involved in a bad deal

Comfort me when things don't look good

Comfort me when I need to be understood

Comfort me with your soft words

Comfort me with your sweet voice

Comfort me when I do not have a choice

Comfort me so you can be my queen

Comfort me knowing that I am your only king

Comfort me when I've walked the last mile of the way

Comfort me when things don't look good

Comfort me for the rest of my life

Comfort me when I feel depressed

Comfort me when I need rest

Comfort me when I need sleep

Comfort me in times of trouble

Comfort me!

Comfort me!

Comfort me!

For Some Reason

For some reason, when you're not around,

I can hear the echoes of your empty voice

Beating against my vacant and shattered mind

For some reason, the times we are apart,

I truly miss you

For some reason, I want you to know that

I'm trapped inside this bubble of love

For some reason, I wish you were a bottle, and I was smoke

I would slide through the door of your lips

And lay next to your warm heart

For some reason, I know it's too late

But life goes on

My love for you keeps on burning over and over again

Oh! how I love you

For some reason, the weight of your love seems so heavy when you are around

For some reason, I'm still in love with you

For some reason.

Give Me More

I've been holding on to these liquid bars built from my tears
I'm holding to my emotions, never letting them go
Like a doorframe that encases the door
I can't forget the look in your eyes
that reminds me of the sun that shines as it hangs over the eastern shore
Please, my darling, come back where you belong
and take your time and love me slowly
I can feel your love flowing inside of me like salt across the sea
My emotions are flying like the wings of a honey bee,
I want you to have all of me
This love that you're giving me, I never had before,
Please don't stop; just give me more
You have drained my body; it does not feel the same
I can feel your hot love running through my veins
This love you're giving me seems to take away the pain,
Darling, your love is special and strange
It has me dangling on a string
This love I never had before
Please don't stop; just give me more.

Honestly

Honestly, honestly, from the other side of my heart, which is the deepest side

I think of you, my love

Like the sun gives light so we will not be in darkness

But the times you lay your face on my chest, as if it was your own personal pillow

Honestly, honestly, I can feel our hearts and minds beating together as an orchestra

Every musical instrument is playing our love song

I really enjoy being in love with you

I don't mind doing it over and over again

You turned out to be my best friend

There is this connection between you and me

Honestly, honestly

Your love feels like heaven trapped inside my soul

Sometimes, I grip my fist only to touch what's inside

Honestly, honestly

I want to slowly drift asleep imagining, wishing my dreams would become my cruise ship

I just couldn't help myself when I fell in love with you

You are my goddess

I feel every fraction of your love

Honestly! Honestly!

I Can't Stop Myself From Loving You

From Loving You

I can't stop myself from loving you

I feel like a feather floating in gravity

Lost in space

Since you took your love away, this world has become a very lonely place

This emotional suitcase I must carry

This weight I don't want to bear

My heart beats in pain every single second

But I still must pack this emotional suitcase

No one else seems to care

My heart collapsed the last time you embraced me

Your beautiful face I can't replace

Oh, my darling! Oh, my darling!

I want to love you so deeply

I could never feel the pain, even if you didn't love me back

I just can't stop myself from loving you.

I Could Never

I could never engage in another relationship with someone else
I could never think of loving outside of your heart
I could never hear a voice more pleasant than yours
I could never see beauty in the face of another
I could never inhale the scent of another sweeter than yours
I could never touch lips softer than yours
I could never close my eyes to kiss another
That would violate our code of love
I could never lay against a smoother skin than yours
I could never force myself into a stranger love bank
That could not guarantee a withdrawal of love
I could never feel guilty because I love with no shame
Believe me, I could never.

I Feel Your Love

I feel your love resting on the loveseat of my mind

Only if you would kiss me under the comfort of the stars until the sun refuses to shine

I have been arrested by my own sentiment

You have given me freedom

I'm thankful for your approachable personality

Your adorable face has given a resting place for the polestar of my eyes

All the angels above are crying as they watch us love each other through the windows in the sky

I feel your love

They're waving their handkerchiefs as a witness that one would say goodbye

Oh, my love,

I love you so much

That my pen spoke to me from the bottom of the ink

Only to write about my love for you

How it was born from the crimson-patched moon

From the semen-gray clouds,

I feel your love

On the night that I whispered

Through the entrance of your ear,

The moment I told you that I love you,

I wanted to bury my love in the deepest safe of your heart

For sure, I need you more than a clock needs time

I feel your love.

I Keep Reminding Myself

I keep reminding myself time after time how much I love you
The edges of my heart have worn out
When I heard that you were leaving, I became distraught,
Knowing my nerves have been shaken to pieces
Your face is as beautiful as a landscape of roses
Hanging from the boulders of my eyes
Every time you touch me, I shake like a wet, wounded, cold bird
Your touch melts the mantle of my frozen heart
Your love has built a castle around my mind
I will forever be lost in time
I stand on the walls and scream out your name,
Hoping you will hear my call
My thoughts start playing games inside my head
Without you, I'm as good as dead
I keep reminding myself over and over again
How much I love you
I keep reminding myself.

I Never Met a Dream

Where are you?

I'm so hungry for your presence

Last night, I almost drowned in my tears

I didn't know that the hunger of wanting to be loved by you could hurt so severe

The beauty of you walks inside my mind

You're something special

And I need you all the time

I never met a true dream that I ever needed so much

How badly I want your touch

It seems as if you belong to me

The texture of your lips is a mystery to see

I need you, and you need me

Trying unsuccessfully to ignore my desires

The idea of loving you really sets my heart on fire

I never met a dream

Yet now I think I did.

I Want You

I want you, oh my love
These emotions seem to be getting the best of me
I'm living my life through a dream that has come true
All I want to do is constantly show you how much I love you
I see the magic in your eyes
The compassion in your tears
You're absolutely beautiful
And easy to love
Oh, my love
These feelings I have for you
Cannot be denied
I'm willing to let go of any pride
I don't like the idea of saying goodnight
Knowing I must live tonight without you
Tell me, my love, what am I going to do without you?
I want you in my wildest dreams
I never thought I would be in love with you
You have turned my world upside down
Oh, my love, Oh, my love
I want you
Tell me, my love
Tell me, what am I going to do without you
I want you like a single lonely man who is waiting at the end to be loved
How can you live life knowing I need you
Oh, my love
Oh, my love
I want you forever and ever
Let's die together
I want you.

I Want You Here

I want you here with me. It feels so good.
Oh! My love, can I look into your lonely eyes to tell you how much I love you?
My emotional flames are burning out of control.
Because you are not speaking to me,
There are broken pieces of my love lying all over the floor of my heart.
I can't stop myself from loving you.
I just can't. I just can't.
The more I pull away, the deeper my love for you mourns.
I thought you and I would always love each other in our own way.
I'm still in love with you.
I think of you day and night.
Life is meaningless without you.
The times we are not talking, I try to make myself happy.
I want you to know that I will always love you.
The moments you are away, I sing love tunes every minute of the day.
I can't stop thinking about you, no matter how hard I try.
I keep telling myself that you will always be the apple of my eye.
Sometimes, I wish we could undo the past,
Only to spend the rest of my days loving you.
I want you here with me.

I'm in Love With You

I discovered something

There are times I feel so depressed

Knowing I'm not able to express the way I feel

As a matter of fact

I love you

Considerably more

I really do

The times I can't see you

causes stress to attack my mind

This love vine that has overpowered me

The fruit of pain seems to hang inside my starving heart

As long as I know you exist

I could never be free from these emotions locked inside of me

I love you so much

What am I to do?

My heart refuses to give me rest

Often, I tell myself I do not like you anymore

Nevertheless,

I'm so in love with you.

I'm Madly in Love With You

Did you know I'm madly in love with you?

Just the thought of you not loving me back terrifies me

Repeatedly asking myself how this happened to me

Tell me, my love, exactly how did you lock your love inside of my silent tears

Like a broken vessel, all my tears escaped and ran down my face

I started chasing behind the deep, powerful footprints of love

Only to find myself back to my leaking heart

Did you know that I'm madly in love with you?

Just One More Time

Is there any space in your heart to love me just one more time?

After all you and I have gone through,

I'll do anything to make it up to you

Give me, my love, just one more chance

I need this opportunity

It would mean the world to me

Just one more time

I just want to mend the pain

I'm thinking about the positivity in life

that I can gain if you love me the way I love you

If things were turned around, you would ask the same

Tell me, my love,

is there any space in your heart to love me?

Just one more time

I'll never stop trying

It's almost done

Don't know how long I can hold on

Is there any space in your heart to love me?

Just one more time.

Listen to My Voice

Patiently, I walked through the stillness of the silent night
Since the day I met you, I haven't found rest in my soul
My love for you has made me sick
When I lay my body down on my bed,
If only I could sleep the night away
Something about your gravitating love has turned me inside out
My love for you makes me want to scream and shout
There is no doubt I desire everything about you
The way you have apprehended my tender, concealed heart
Don't hurt my feelings
By not telling me you love me back
Come, my love,
I want to kiss you
As an infant will cling to his mother's breast,
May I embrace every part of you
Let me load my emotions upon your heart
Until death, we do part
Listen to my voice
I love you.

My Tears

My tears are proof that I love you

My tears remind me how lost I am without you

My tears are like precious pearls buried in the depths of the sea

Hoping someone like you would find me

My tears talk to my heart being tormented by your absence

My tears are proof that you are everything that I've ever wanted or need by my side

My tears!

Only

Only if you knew my love for you is like a wild, flaming fire burning out of control

Only your hands that drip with perfume wander over me

Only the kiss of your lips I always miss

Only your wet kiss reminds me of the sweetest glass of dinner wine

Only your soft skin that stays so warm comforts me in a storm

Only you can make me feel the way I do

Only you know how much I really love you

Only with you, every minute ticks quickly away

Only the moments that you are away make every hour seem like a day

Only my love that falls like rain can release the pain when I think of your name Only!

I will wait for you.

Only!

I have words of love for you

Only loving you is more than a dream

I cannot turn back

Only! I can love you

To the end.

Only If I Had Wings

I have been touched by your love

The perpetual shadows of your love won't leave me alone

I really love you today more than ever before

Only if I had wings to soar high through the sky,
searching for a place to land, hopefully

Upon your sweet cranberry lips

To drink the moisture from your wet kisses

Only if I had wings.

Please Forgive Me

Please forgive me for falling in love with you
The power of your love came down like a waterfall pouring into my heart
Like the flood that surrounded Noah's ark
What an enormous feeling knowing I can't speak to you or touch you
It's tearing me apart
Lay here in solitary
Looking into space, hoping I could see your face
It is only fair to me that you should know that I love you so
Believe me
Unexpectedly, this loveliness just overtook me
I really can't help the way I feel
Will you please forgive me?
Please forgive me
For falling in love with you
I couldn't help myself.

Set Me Free

Just in a period of time

All my hopes and dreams drifted away
like a boat at sea

It seems so hard

I'm having a conflict with not being loved
begging to be set free

All alone

I am tired and weak

I have dropped to my lowest peak
hanging the love that once was strong

Four or five times a day.

I have to wipe my tears away

I must have realized that love is a hurting thing,
recalling back in the past when I thought your love would last

When love is locked inside one's heart,
the giver goes through pain

While the taker gets the love and plays the game,
the giver suffers through the pain

Being locked by the passionate chain,
the taker has the key to love.

The Bars of Love

Again, the bars of love have surrounded me

The quiet passion is so loud that no one can hear my pain

Loneliness has wrapped around me

No one knows

I can barely stand on my feet

My life is almost gone

How long can this go on?

Again, the bars of love have captured me

But the truth of the matter is,

I don't want to be free

My love for you is too strong.

These Emotions I Just Love

These emotions of love, I love so much
These emotions of love I live to touch
These emotions of love sink into my ears
These emotions of love, I want to hear
These emotions of love sometimes become my eyes
These emotions of love I need by my side
These emotions of love, I don't want them to go
These emotions of love I never had before
These emotions of love, at times, walk out the door
These emotions of love have me tossing in bed
These emotions of love, I can't get them out of my head
These emotions of love caused me to make mistakes
These emotions of love, at times, caused me to break
These emotions of love, at times, caused me to be mad
These emotions of love, at times, caused me to be sad
These emotions of love, at times, caused me to be glad
These emotions of love, at times, caused me to rack my mind
These emotions of love caused me to forget the importance of time
These emotions!
I just love!

The One You Love Hurts You Most

Why is it that the one you love hurts you most?

Oftentimes, giving to another what really belongs to you

Leaving you not knowing which way to turn

But when will you ever learn?

The one you love hurts you the most

You empty your heart, and you pour out your soul

No one on earth knows how bad you feel

And it will be this way until you find a way to forgive

Can't seem to understand why all my dreams have fallen to the ground For some reason, they can't be found

The one you love hurts you the most

Yes, when you left me, my heart experienced the greatest pain of all

Only to taste the strongest passion that one could feel

Oh my, something has gone wrong

I wonder if I will be able to hold on.

Why?

The one you love hurts you the most.

The Sweet Voice

It was a silent night

I was locked in an empty room filled with loneliness and gloom

Wanting to share my thoughts and deep feelings with someone

But not knowing whom

As time went further on, I decided to pick up the phone

I found myself talking to a young lady who also seemed to be alone

Her words entered my lonely world

Sounding as sweet as she could be

She sounded as if she could give me security

My only choice was to listen to the soft voice

Her words were tender and mild

As though she was a newborn child

Telling her I was searching for a true companion,

Just tired and almost ready to call it quits

The honesty of her words blew my mind to bits

Not knowing how to react, it seemed as if it was a dream and not a fact

I imagined her in my life, maybe someday becoming my wife

Think about the times we could kiss

And I'll flip when her lips approach mine

Too bad

It's just a dream

Yet I enjoyed being with you tonight.

The Times

When I can't see you, I find myself crying from within

There is this vile storm brewing from the depths of my soul

The times I can't see you remind me of

the heat trapped inside a wood-burning stove

I've lost full control

No one can regulate the pressure gauge of my heart that has been broken I can't seem to turn off the switch

These dreams keep popping in my head

There is this tidal wave splashing inside my bed

This happens only at times when I can't feel you.

We Belong Together

I can't imagine not sharing my love with you
When we are under the moonlight,
Your eyes glitter like gold I shiver every time we kiss
I lose control
No one could make me feel this way
The times you have walked away,
I could cry a river
After saying goodbye
But being loved by you brings happiness in my life
We belong together.

What Will Appear On Tomorrow

What will appear on tomorrow?

I will never try to escape from your love

The greatest storm I have ever encountered was the moment you walked out the door

It was very difficult for me to dream anymore

I hate that things are going this way

But I don't know what to say

Why would you walk away?

All the magic that surrounded me has flown through an open door

Tell me how I can pick up the broken pieces that are scattered over the floor

These thoughts keep hanging over the shoulder of my heart

The shadows of your love are really tearing me apart

If only you could babysit the emotions of my mind

Now I'm lying in my bed trying to get you out of my head

It seems as if I have been waiting all my life

I thought you were going to be my wife

You were everything

Now, I'm faced with a broken dream

Things have gotten out of control

Now, I can't adjust the temperature of my soul

I'm sitting here in my sorrow

Not knowing what will appear on tomorrow.

Will You Love Me

Will you love me, my darling, until our life is over?
I want to share my life with you
under the moonlight that burns like an Olympic torch.
All this passion started the moment you anchored your
love in the bottom of my heart
There's not one person on earth who can break us apart.
I'm not just imagining that this is all in my head
I feel like the story of Underdog and Sweet Polly Purebred
My love for you is like a love novel sitting on the bookshelf of my
heart Waiting to be read.
The thought of loving you keeps leaping from deep inside my head
My love, would you understand if I dropped a tear?
I just could not help myself. I'm just a passionate man
hoping that you would hold my hand.
I'm lost in all of my thoughts because I am falling in love with you
Believe me. I have fallen to my feet
Every time you touch me, I'm just that weak.
Will you love me? I could never say good-bye
I will forever need your love
You will always live in my heart
Whether you love me or not
Should I live this life as an unhappy man?
This emotional roller coaster seems to be a delusional lovelornness
I just can't control the fact that I love you more than ever
Will you love me?

You Are Extremely Special

You are extremely special to me
The first day we met, your beautiful brown eyes spoke to me first
I wanted to fall into them and swim upstream to your heart
It's so difficult to find a woman who's faithful and honest
I have no choice but to love you
Your disposition validates your worth,
Which is more precious than gold
You're not just a woman
You are the only one who can control the harness of my soul
My love for you is stronger than time
I love you so much
You almost drive me out of my mind
You're so kind
I find happiness each time you kiss me
Over and over again,
You always find a way to make me smile
By being creative
It seems as if all my love is resting on the bottom of your heart
The times I hug you, I'm only trying to get my love back inside of me
I love to smell your moist ocean breath
It causes my heart to beat like twins
You are extremely special!

You Are My Thoughts

You are my thoughts
My emotions have been torn like unwanted paper
My tears have grown legs and run straight down my face,
Each day, falling lower and lower,
I'm feeling out of place
I think life sometimes seems unfair at the moment
I'm the only one who seems to care
It is so hard for me to say goodbye
Wondering at times, should I break down and cry
I have found serenity in the rocking chair of my soul
Everything I know about you is locked behind the memories of time
Now, I'm lying here, walking through the canal of my mind,
Only if I could build a stairway back to the center of your soul
Because this love I have for you has gotten out of control
I just can't stop myself from loving you
My love is just too strong
Your face is posted on the theater walls of my dream
I can hear the soft, sweet tone of your voice speaking as if there were a small speaker pinned under my skin
Your voice seems to speak through the hunger
I smell your scent moving with the pillow of the clouds
I feel your hands caressing mine
I close my eyes as I lay inside the bedroom of my heart
Looking at the ceiling of my imagination, knowing
I will always be in love with you
Because you are my thoughts.

Your Forgiveness

When you asked me to forgive you,

Somehow, it nourished my brokenness

The deep exposed wounds were healed by your love of forgiveness

Your forgiveness keeps me from traveling alone

Without your forgiveness, I'm just another wounded lover

Starving for true love

Somehow lost in this remote state
hoping to overcome these silent echoes that seem to be hanging in space

Your forgiveness was aimed at the core of my heart

I feel your forgiveness boiling in the middle of my soul

Since the day I met you,

I've not been the same

You asked for forgiveness because of how you were dressed

But to me, what you thought was bad

I found comfort in your efforts to apologize

It's truly an honor to know that there are people who respect others

Your forgiveness was aiming at the core of my heart.

Your Love Gripped

Your love has gripped the emotional bars of my heart
I love it when your breath caresses the walls of my vanishing soul
When you are near,
I can smell your sweet, adorable scent traveling through the valley of my nose
Your love always seems to hang in the attic of my mind
You're as delicate and lovely as a hummingbird
Burying the tip of his beak into the hollow of a beautiful flower
I love looking into your glittering eyes
At the same time, exchanging kisses
As our lips battle for the first place
My love, when I awake from sleep,
You are the first person to come to my mind
I love the affection and endearment that you bring to our world of love
Oh, my love, I care about you
like the wetness trapped inside water
Like four quarters that make a dollar
Did you know that you are approachable with that alluring smile?
You have the most gravitating personality
That is so authentic
The way you dress
Is above all the rest
You are the meaning of the classic
My darling, your love really grips the emotional bar of my heart
Your love gripped me.

Your Love Was Born

Your love was born in the delivery room of my heart

The first time you stared into the dinner room of my soul,

I saw the glory of your love

Shining in the shadow of my face

The passion that overtook me is something
I could not erase.

I fell in love from the light of your penetrating eyes
which left me hypnotized

I had no other choice but to compromise.

The only hope I had was to make sure you would always stay by my side

Oh, my love, if you could look inside my tears,

I want to tell you how much I love you

I dream of holding your soft hands as we walk by the calm blue sea.

Excited about the day,

I would bow down on one knee, asking you to marry me

There are so many nights I fight

I hate to tell you good night

Things just don't feel right

I keep reminding myself that when

Your love was born.

www.ingramcontent.com/pod-product-compliance
Lightning Source LLC
LaVergne TN
LVHW041600070526
838199LV00046B/2075